The Detox

KITCHEN

The Detox KITCHEN

*Feel-good food for
happy and healthy eating*

This edition published by Parragon Books Ltd in 2016
and distributed by

Parragon Inc.
440 Park Avenue South, 13th Floor
New York, NY 10016
www.parragon.com/lovefood

LOVE FOOD is an imprint of Parragon Books Ltd

ISBN 978-1-4748-1760-8

Printed in China

New recipes and introduction by Judith Wills
Cover and new recipe photography by Tony Briscoe

NOTES FOR THE READER

This book uses standard kitchen measuring spoons and cups.
All spoon and cup measurements are level unless otherwise
indicated. Unless otherwise stated, milk is assumed to be
whole, eggs are large, individual fruits and vegetables are
medium, and pepper is freshly ground black pepper. Unless
otherwise stated, all root vegetables should be peeled prior
to using.

The times given are only an approximate guide. Preparation
times differ according to the techniques used by different
people and the cooking times may also vary from those given.

Please note that any ingredients stated as being optional
are not included in the nutritional values provided. The
nutritional values given are approximate and provided as only
a guideline; they do not account for individual cooking skills,
measurement equipment, and portion sizes. The nutritional
values provided are per serving or per item.

While the publisher of the book and the original author(s)
of the recipes and other text have made all reasonable
efforts to ensure that the information contained in this book
is accurate and up to date at the time of publication, anyone
reading this book should note the following important points:
* Medical and pharmaceutical knowledge is constantly
changing and the author(s) and the publisher cannot and
do not guarantee the accuracy or appropriateness of the
contents of this book;
* In any event, this book is not intended to be, and should
not be relied upon, as a substitute for appropriate, tailored
professional advice. Both the author(s) and the publisher
strongly recommend that a physician or other healthcare
professional is consulted before embarking on major
dietary changes;
* For the reasons set out above, and to the fullest extent
permitted by law, the author(s) and publisher: (i) cannot
and do not accept any legal duty of care or responsibility in
relation to the accuracy or appropriateness of the contents
of this book, even where expressed as "advice" or using
other words to this effect; and (ii) disclaim any liability,
loss, damage, or risk that may be claimed or incurred as
a consequence—directly or indirectly—of the use and/or
application of any of the contents of this book.

WHY DETOX YOUR DIET?

Most of us are aware that health and well-being are strongly linked with what we eat—and with what we don't eat. Many minor, and more serious, illnesses and everyday health problems can be prevented, improved, or even eliminated by choosing the right diet. For example, two of the major health issues of today, obesity and type-2 diabetes, are closely linked with food intake, and heart disease, many types of cancer, arthritis, and dementia are all thought to be at least in part affected by diet as well.

Research continues to prove that day-to-day energy, vitality, mood, and brain function can be improved through food choices. Our appearance can also be enhanced by what we eat or choose to avoid. Healthy skin, hair, eyes, gums, and nails are largely dependent on a good diet.

Despite all these fantastic potential benefits for choosing a healthy diet, many people still feel that making the necessary changes will be too hard. One reason may be because, for many years, the term "detox" has been used to describe a process of rethinking what we eat and drink in order to "cleanse" our bodies, in particular, the liver and digestive system.

For many people, the term "detox" indicates drastic, short-term changes, usually combined with a particularly low intake of calories. The idea of a detox diet can seem extreme and something that you would want to avoid doing for any length of time.

However, this book sets out to show you a different, more gentle and user-friendly way to cleanse your body and to rethink the way you feel about detoxing. This method is better for the body and provides a more healthy diet to give it the best possible chance to feel healthy, revitalized, toxin-free, and running at optimum efficiency.

The recipes in this book are all easy to follow and the ingredients are easy to find, being widely available in most supermarkets or health food stores. The results are designed to delight your taste buds, satisfy your appetite, and provide an exciting variety of flavors and textures. Most of the recipes are extremely family-friendly, so all of the family can enjoy the benefits of this clean way of eating, without having to make separate detox meals for one person.

The detox lifestyle that you will enjoy here is something you can—and will want to—follow every day for the rest of your life. It is not restrictive or boring, but contains meals that you will look forward to making and experimenting with. Because the ingredients are often healthy, there is no need to feel hungry either, unlike with other diets.

WHAT IS A DETOX DIET?

Our detox recipes avoid using certain ingredients that are most often linked to causing adverse reactions within our bodies as well as health and well-being problems. The foods this book avoid are:

WHEAT AND OTHER GLUTEN-CONTAINING GRAINS
While only a small percentage of people have celiac disease, a serious allergy to gluten, the number is growing and people who experience nonceliac gluten sensitivity (NCGS) have similar symptoms. Other people show sensitivity to wheat. A diet high in wheat and refined grains has also been linked with obesity and high blood sugar levels.

REFINED SUGAR
Numerous studies from across the world have found a link between refined sugar consumption and obesity, diabetes, poor dental health, and cardiovascular disease. The World Health Organization (WHO) recently recommended a drastic reduction in our refined sugar intake.

DAIRY FOODS
Two-thirds of the adult population of the world cannot digest lactose, a component of dairy milk, properly, according to the U.S. National Library of Medicine. Cow milk consumption has also been linked to acne, some cancers, inflammation, and other health problems.

PROCESSED FOODS
Foods that have gone through an intensive manufacturing process tend to contain unhealthy additives, as well as being high in salt, sugar, fats, and potential toxins.

ALCOHOL
Long-term or high intake of alcohol can cause high blood pressure, heart disease, strokes, liver disease, and digestive problems, as well as depression, insomnia, dementia, and many other health issues.

RED MEAT
Consumption of red meat, such as beef, pork, and lamb, and processed and smoked meats, is linked with an increased risk of some cancers and heart disease, as well as inflammation and damage to the digestive system. A high animal protein diet may also cause kidney problems.

TOO MUCH SODIUM
A high-sodium diet is linked with an increased risk of high blood pressure, as well as with fluid retention, and may make symptoms of several conditions, including asthma and arthritis, worse.

CAFFEINE
Caffeine-rich beverages, such as coffee, tea, and cola, are linked with insomnia, nervousness, panic attacks, irritability, increased heart rate, and stomach upsets and also tend to raise blood sugar levels.

WHAT YOU CAN EAT ON A DETOX DIET

Our detox recipes will help you to eat a diet that contains all the nutrients you need for health and well-being. You will not be going short on carbohydrates, protein, or fats, and the foods featured are bursting with natural health-giving plant chemicals, vitamins, minerals, and fiber. The recipes are also packed with foods known to boost your immune system, increase "friendly" bacteria in the digestive tract, and assist the liver, which is the main detoxifying organ of the body. Here are some of the important food groups in our recipes:

FRUITS AND VEGETABLES

Fruits and vegetables will form a large part of any detox diet. They provide healthy carbohydrates, fiber, plant chemicals, and vitamin C. Many types of fruits and vegetables, such as beets, lemons, those in the cabbage family, apples, celery, and artichokes, are also known to support liver function and to promote a healthy digestive tract.

NUTS AND SEEDS

Nuts and seeds are rich in healthy fats and are a great source of nonanimal protein, minerals, and vitamins. They are extremely versatile ingredients and form an important part of a detox diet. They are also useful for snacking on to stave off hunger.

LEGUMES

Legumes, such as lentils and dried beans, are one of the best plant sources of protein. They also contain fiber-rich carbohydrates, plant chemicals for health protection, and vitamins and minerals. They are easily added to stews and casseroles to boost the nutritional value of a meal.

WHOLE GRAINS

Even if you are avoiding wheat, rye, barley, and oats in your diet, you can still enjoy a wide range of grains and grainlike plants that are known to be suitable for gluten and wheat–sensitive people. In this book, we use some of these tasty health–packed grains, such as quinoa, buckwheat, and cornmeal.

DAIRY ALTERNATIVES

Food products produced from almond, hazelnut, coconut, rice, and soy are easily digested and ideal to replace standard dairy foods in the diet. They can be made into milks, yogurts, creams, and butters and provide easy substitutions for dairy products.

OILY FISH

Oily fish is rich in vital omega–3 fats, which offer health protection in many ways. So it is good to include oily fish, such as salmon, herring, mackerel, and sardines, on a detox plan to provide vital fats in your diet.

MAKING GOOD CHOICES

In your everyday detox diet, it is important to make good choices when choosing ingredients. Examples of this are oils and seasonings. For cooking oils, you can choose several types of plant-base oils, but there are a few points to keep in mind.

Remember that many plant oils have a low smoking point, which means that if you use them to cook at high temperatures, their healthy fats can oxidize and become unhealthy. Olive oil—particularly cold-pressed and extra virgin olive oil—has a fairly low smoke point, so cook with it over low or medium heat for as short a time as possible. Canola oil and coconut oil have a higher smoke point, so they are more suitable for cooking at higher temperatures.

For salads, all of the plant, seed, and nut oils can create fantastic dressings, being rich in healthy fats and vitamin E. Try to use cold-pressed or extra virgin oils in salads, because they contain highest levels of health-protective plant chemicals. Olive, canola, and hazelnut oil are great sources of monounsaturated fats, while flaxseed oil, hempseed oil, walnut oil, and canola oil contain good amounts of omega-3 fats.

To cut down on salt and sodium, there are plenty of alternative seasonings available to people on a detox diet. When omitting salt, it helps to use plenty of other alternative flavorings to provide zest, interest, and flavor. Herbs are indispensible. Soft herbs, such as basil, parsley, tarragon, and cilantro leaf, can be used as they are, stirred in or on top of a dish. Other firmer herbs, such as rosemary, bay leaves, and thyme, are ideal in cooked dishes.

Fresh and dried spices can be used to enhance almost any dish, and all herbs and spices are rich in plant chemicals and antioxidants while some, including cinnamon and turmeric, are liver-supporting and form an important part of any detox plan. Don't forget juices, such as lime, lemon, and orange juices, which are great in salad dressings. Many types of vinegar, from sweet balsamic to sherry, apple cider, and rice vinegars, are ideal for dressings and cooked dishes and some are thought to be digestive aids.

You can add sweetness to detox dishes in a variety of ways. Most fruits—dried, fresh, pureed, or chopped—are ideal, and they also add bulk, nutrients, fiber, and flavor. Unrefined sugars, such as coconut palm sugar and molasses, offer a high level of sweetness and also flavor. Molasses is rich in iron and other minerals. Syrups can also be a good choice for sweetening—from maple syrup to date syrup, as well as agave nectar and brown rice syrup. These syrups also tend to have a minimal impact on blood sugars. Raw honey can be another good choice, because it has antiseptic qualities and, again, adds flavor and sweetening to any dish.

Try to buy organic, raw, and unrefined produce whenever you can, if possible, for maximum health benefits on a detox diet.

DETOX
FOR HEALTH

There is much research to show that your health, your well-being, and your lifespan can be improved by eating more of the healthy foods that are described on page 11 and fewer of the foods that are described on page 8. In essence, following this food balance is what we mean by "detoxing," and it will give your body—including the detoxing organs the liver, kidneys, skin, and lungs, as well as the lymphatic and digestive systems—the best chance to work optimally, helping your body to be healthy, free from disease and functioning as you want it to.

Featured below are the main benefits that people notice when they follow a balanced detoxing way of eating, such as we have described in this book. These benefits will probably become more obvious and more pronounced over time:

~ Weight loss
~ Reduction in fluid retention
~ Improved digestive function
~ Increased energy
~ Better sleep
~ Better skin
~ Improved mood—less chance of depression and anxiety.

There are important other long-term health benefits, too. You may reduce your risk of getting several major diseases, including heart disease, cancers; type-2 diabetes, arthritis, and dementia, and a detox diet can reduce the severity of some of the symptoms. Some people who have type 2 diabetes may even find that it will eventually disappear.

You can boost the effects of your gentle long-term detox by getting regular, moderate exercise—for example, take a 20–30-minute walk on most days, increasing your pace as you become used to it. Exercise has also been shown to help rid the body of harmful chemicals. Moderate exercise encourages the lungs to work harder (by increasing your heart rate) and stimulates all of the detoxing organs so that they also function more effectively.

Remember to drink enough fluids when on a detox diet. Plain water is ideal but juices and smoothies are also good in moderation. Keeping well hydrated will help to make sure that your digestive system, liver, and kidneys function well.

QUESTIONS AND ANSWERS ABOUT DETOX

Q: WILL I FEEL HUNGRY?

A: No. If you eat and drink regularly and choose a variety of meals and snacks from our recipes, you will not be reducing your calories so low that you feel hungry. And, of course, you can always add in extra snacks, such as nuts, seeds, nondairy yogurt, and raw vegetables, if you do feel hungry between meals. Such a diet will be high in fiber and low on the glycemic index, two important factors in reducing hunger.

Q: CAN I DETOX IF I AM ESPECIALLY PHYSICALLY ACTIVE?

A: Yes. You simply need to make sure that you eat enough calories so that you have plenty of energy to see you safely through your active lifestyle. Meals and snacks containing good amounts of carbohydrates (check the nutrition panels in this book) are ideal to eat before and after exercise, as well as fruit and nuts for snacking, if needed.

Q: WHAT IS THE DIFFERENCE BETWEEN DETOX AND A CRASH DIET?

A: Crash diets are usually extremely low in calories and tend to focus on a limited number of foods. Our detox recipes do not require you to do either of these things, because we aim for a longer-term change of habits.

Q: IS IT HARD TO FIND THE INGREDIENTS FOR THE DETOX RECIPES?

A: No. We have made sure that all the ingredients are widely available in supermarkets or health food stores.

Q: WILL A DETOX EATING PLAN BE EXPENSIVE?

A: It certainly does not have to be. While some of the ingredients are more expensive than others, many are low in cost and easily available from a wide variety of sources. You will also save money by avoiding expensive or unnecessary items that are not part of a detox diet, such as red meat, alcohol, and processed snacks. Shopping wisely and choosing fresh produce that is in season will also help you to save.

Q: IS THE DETOX DIET SAFE TO FOLLOW?

A: Yes, it is safe. If you follow our guidelines and recipes, you will be choosing a healthy way to eat, which will also give your body's natural "detoxing" mechanisms, particularly the liver, as much support as possible. However, it is essential to consult your physician before starting the diet if you have any special health issues or particular concerns.

BREAKFASTS AND JUICES

Raw carrot, apple, and goji bircher muesli	20
Date and chia pudding	22
Spiced quinoa porridge with berries	24
Baked eggs with asparagus	26
Smashed avocado with toasted hemp seeds	28
Spicy black bean and corn scramble with toasted polenta	30
Kale and banana smoothie	32
Beet and Swiss chard juice	34
Green tea juice	36
Carrot and cucumber juice	38
Spinach energy booster juice	40
Tantalizing tomato juice	42

RAW CARROT, APPLE, AND GOJI BIRCHER MUESLI

Buckwheat grains are soaked overnight for easy digestion and packed with plenty of other healthy ingredients to create a delicious, good-for-you version of Swiss bircher muesli.

SERVES: 4

PREP: 15 MINS, PLUS OVERNIGHT SOAKING   COOK: NONE

3 cups buckwheat flakes
1 carrot, grated
2 red-skinned apples
²/₃ cup apple juice
²/₃ cup almond milk
1½ tablespoons dried goji berries
2 tablespoons chopped hazelnuts
2 tablespoons dried chopped apricots
1½ tablespoons shelled pistachio nuts
1 tablespoon sunflower seeds

1. Put the buckwheat flakes and carrot into a large bowl. Core, thinly slice, and chop one of the apples and add to the bowl. Stir the bowl contents well until thoroughly combined. Stir in the apple juice, almond milk, and 1 tablespoon of the goji berries. Cover and let stand overnight in the refrigerator.

2. Stir the hazelnuts into the bowl. Core, thinly slice, and chop the remaining apple.

3. Divide the muesli among serving dishes and sprinkle the apple, remaining goji berries, apricots, pistachio nuts, and sunflower seeds over the muesli. Serve immediately.

MILK ALTERNATIVE
If you prefer a creamier option, you can use all almond milk to soak the flakes instead of using apple juice.

PER SERVING: 260 CALS | 7G FAT | 0.7G SAT FAT | 47G CARBS | 18.3G SUGARS | 7.3G FIBER | 6.7G PROTEIN | TRACE SODIUM

DATE AND CHIA PUDDING

Chia seeds, when soaked overnight in coconut milk, make a wonderfully silky-smooth dish that is high in healthy fats and ideal for an elegant breakfast with little preparation.

SERVES: 2

PREP: 10 MINS, PLUS OVERNIGHT SOAKING   COOK: NONE

3 tablespoons chia seeds
1 cup coconut milk
1½ teaspoons date syrup
seeds from ½ vanilla bean
3 tablespoons coconut soy yogurt
1 large medjool date, chopped
½ orange, sliced
1 tablespoon pomegranate seeds

1. Place the chia seeds, coconut milk, date syrup, and vanilla seeds in a large bowl. Stir thoroughly to combine. Transfer to a container, cover, and let soak overnight in the refrigerator.

2. When ready to serve, divide the chia mixture among serving bowls. Spread the coconut yogurt over the top of each dish, then top with the date, orange slices, and pomegranate seeds.

3. Serve immediately.

CHEERS FOR CHIA
Chia seeds are rich in omega-3 fatty acids, fiber, and minerals and their nutrients are easily absorbed by the body.

PER SERVING: 226 CALS | 12.6G FAT | 6.6G SAT FAT | 26.3G CARBS | 14.9G SUGARS | 8.4G FIBER | 5.1G PROTEIN | 40MG SODIUM

SPICED QUINOA PORRIDGE WITH BERRIES

High in protein and fiber, quinoa flakes make a perfect start to the day, and they will keep any hunger pangs at bay until lunchtime.

SERVES: 4
PREP: 5 MINS COOK: 6 MINS

1 cup quinoa flakes
1 tablespoon ground flaxseed
½ teaspoon sea salt
½ teaspoon ground cinnamon
¼ teaspoon ground ginger
¼ teaspoon ground nutmeg
2 cups almond milk
1 tablespoon agave nectar
2 tablespoons goldenberries
3 tablespoons dry unsweetened coconut flakes
⅓ cup fresh blueberries
⅓ cup fresh raspberries
⅓ cup fresh blackberries

1. In a large bowl, combine the quinoa flakes, flaxseed, salt, and spices.

2. Heat the almond milk in a saucepan and add the quinoa flake mixture. Stir and bring to a simmer, then add the agave nectar. Cook, stirring frequently, for about 6 minutes, or until you have a thick porridge and the flakes are soft. Add a little extra milk or water if you prefer a thinner porridge, and stir in well.

3. Ladle the porridge into serving bowls and top each with one-quarter of the goldenberries, coconut flakes, and fresh berries. Serve immediately.

GORGEOUS GOLDENBERRIES

Goldenberries are dried Cape gooseberries — this fruit is also known as Chinese lanterns, or ground cherries.

PER SERVING: 198 CALS | 6.1G FAT | 1.8G SAT FAT | 29.8G CARBS | 10.4G SUGARS | 6.1G FIBER | 4.9G PROTEIN | 360MG SODIUM

BAKED EGGS
WITH ASPARAGUS

Protein-rich eggs retain their rightful place on the breakfast table—and pairing them with vitamin- and fiber-rich asparagus provides a healthy, tasty treat.

SERVES: 2
PREP: 10 MINS COOK: 12 MINS

1¼ tablespoons extra virgin canola oil
½ teaspoon paprika
1 garlic clove, crushed
¼ teaspoon sea salt
¼ teaspoon pepper
12 asparagus spears, tough ends removed
4 eggs
1 tomato, seeded and diced
1 tablespoon snipped fresh chives

1. Preheat the oven to 375°F. In a small bowl, combine 1 tablespoon of the oil with all but a pinch of the paprika. Thoroughly stir in the garlic, salt, and pepper.

2. Coat the asparagus spears thoroughly in the flavored oil, then place in two shallow gratin dishes. Roast in the preheated oven for 7 minutes, or until nearly tender when pierced with a sharp knife.

3. Crack the eggs evenly over the asparagus and drizzle with any remaining seasoned oil. Return to the oven for 5 minutes, or until the whites are set and the yolks are still runny.

4. Serve the eggs and asparagus with the diced tomatoes and chives sprinkled over the top. Drizzle with the remaining ¼ tablespoon canola oil and garnish with the remaining pinch of paprika.

FRESHER THE BETTER
Try to be sure that the eggs you use are fresh, so that the whites do not spread too much across the asparagus when you crack them into the dish.

PER SERVING: 252 CALS | 18.5G FAT | 3.7G SAT FAT | 7.2G CARBS | 3.4G SUGARS | 3.3G FIBER | 15.2G PROTEIN | 440MG SODIUM

SMASHED AVOCADO WITH TOASTED HEMP SEEDS

This great combination of avocado and hemp seeds gives you a perfect balance of fats and a wide range of plant chemicals.

SERVES: 2
PREP: 5 MINS COOK: 1–2 MINS

2 tablespoons raw hemp seeds
2 ripe avocados, coarsely chopped
1 tablespoon lemon juice
1½ teaspoons extra virgin olive oil
1 large garlic clove, crushed
½ teaspoon sea salt
½ teaspoon pepper
2 thick slices gluten–free
whole–grain bread, toasted
½ fresh red chile, seeded and finely chopped,
to garnish

1. Put a small, nonstick skillet over medium heat. Add the hemp seeds and toast for 1–2 minutes, then set aside in a small dish.

2. Put the avocado into a large bowl. Add the lemon juice, oil, garlic, salt, pepper, and 1½ tablespoons of the toasted hemp seeds. Stir to combine, then mash to a coarse puree.

3. Serve on the whole–grain toast, sprinkled with the remaining hemp seeds and the chopped chile.

TIME-SAVING TIP
If you want to save a little time at breakfast, you can prepare the avocado mixture the evening before. Just level the surface of the mixture and pour over a thin layer of olive oil to stop the fruit from browning.

PER SERVING: 464 CALS | 32.3G FAT | 4.1G SAT FAT | 38.8G CARBS | 3G SUGARS | 13.6G FIBER | 8.8G PROTEIN | 270MG SODIUM

SPICY BLACK BEAN AND CORN SCRAMBLE WITH TOASTED POLENTA

A Mexican-inspired version of scrambled eggs, served with Italian polenta as toast, this provides a marvelous weekend breakfast or brunch.

SERVES: 2
PREP: 10 MINS, PLUS RESTING   COOK: 20 MINS

½ cup fine yellow cornmeal
1 teaspoon low-sodium, gluten-free
vegetable bouillon powder
1 tablespoon nutritional yeast flakes
½ teaspoon sea salt
1 tablespoon extra virgin canola oil,
plus 1 teaspoon for brushing
2½ tablespoons finely chopped red onion
3 tablespoons finely chopped red bell pepper
1 small garlic clove, crushed
3 tablespoons corn kernels, cooked and rinsed
3 tablespoons black beans, cooked and rinsed
1 teaspoon sugar-free chili sauce
4 eggs, beaten

1. Line a 6-inch square shallow dish or baking pan with parchment paper.

2. Make the Italian polenta at least 2 hours before you want to toast it. Put the cornmeal into a small bowl. Bring 1½ cups of water to a boil in a saucepan with the vegetable bouillon powder and when it is rapidly boiling, gradually pour in the cornmeal, stirring all the time. Continue cooking and stirring over high heat for 3 minutes, until it thickens. Turn the heat down, stir in the nutritional yeast and salt, and simmer, stirring frequently, until you have a thick paste.

3. Spoon the cornmeal mixture into the prepared dish or pan. Cover with plastic wrap or aluminum foil and place in the refrigerator for 2 hours, or until firm. Cut into four triangles.

4. Add half of the oil to a small skillet and put over medium heat. Cook the onion and bell pepper for 7 minutes, or until soft. Stir in the garlic, corn, beans, and chili sauce and cook for an additional minute. Set aside and keep warm.

5. Preheat a ridged grill pan or the broiler to medium. Lightly brush the polenta triangles with the 1 teaspoon of oil and grill or broil until turning golden and flecked dark brown. Turn over and cook the other side.

6. In a separate, small skillet, add the remaining oil and put over medium heat. Add the eggs and cook, stirring with a spatula or wooden spoon from time to time, until lightly scrambled. Gently stir the bean mixture into the eggs and serve with the toasted polenta.

PER SERVING: 427 CALS | 19.9G FAT | 4G SAT FAT | 43.2G CARBS | 2.4G SUGARS | 3.9G FIBER | 19G PROTEIN | 1,080MG SODIUM

KALE AND BANANA SMOOTHIE

This creamy smoothie tastes like an indulgent treat—however, it is actually good for you!

SERVES: 1
PREP: 5 MINS COOK: NONE

½ cup coarsely chopped curly green kale
1 cup chilled water
1 teaspoon hemp seeds or hemp seed oil
1 small banana, frozen
1 teaspoon raw cacao powder,
plus ⅛ teaspoon to garnish
¼ vanilla bean, seeds scraped

1. Put the chopped kale into a blender with the measured water and blend until smooth.

2. Add the hemp seeds, banana, cacao, and vanilla seeds, and blend again until smooth and creamy. Serve immediately, with the raw cacao to garnish.

BANANA BLITZ
To freeze bananas, first peel them, then freeze on a tray for 30 minutes, spaced well apart. When frozen, transfer to plastic food bags or containers. Use within 3–4 months.

PER SERVING: 133 CALS | 2.4G FAT | 0.4G SAT FAT | 28.1G CARBS | 13.1G SUGARS | 5.1G FIBER | 4.3G PROTEIN | TRACE SODIUM

BEET AND
SWISS CHARD JUICE

*This thirst-quenching, nutrient-packed juice
is bursting with vitamins and minerals.*

SERVES: 1
PREP: 5 MINS   COOK: NONE

1 beet, halved
½ lime
1 cup coarsely chopped red Swiss chard
about ⅛ watermelon, thickly sliced
and peel removed
small handful of ice (optional)

1. Feed the beet and lime, then the Swiss chard and watermelon, through a juicer.

2. Fill a glass halfway with ice (if using), then pour in the juice and serve immediately.

BEETS ARE BEST
Beets contains virtually all the
vitamins and minerals needed to give
your whole body a boost.

PER SERVING: 216 CALS | 1.1G FAT | 0.1G SAT FAT | 53.1G CARBS | 40.2G SUGARS | 5.9G FIBER | 5.9G PROTEIN | 200MG SODIUM

GREEN TEA
JUICE

Green tea is packed with antioxidants. Combined with ginseng and wheatgrass, it is a great detoxifying juice that will cleanse you from the inside out.

SERVES: 1
PREP: 5 MINS COOK: NONE

1¼ cups green tea
juice of ½ lemon
¼ teaspoon liquid ginseng
1 teaspoon pea protein
1 teaspoon wheatgrass powder
1 teaspoon maca powder
ice cubes, to serve

1. Whisk the green tea with the lemon juice, ginseng, pea protein, wheatgrass powder, and maca powder. Alternatively, you can combine the ingredients in a blender.

2. Serve immediately over ice.

PARTY PUNCH
To cater for a summer party or a backyard party with friends, scale up the recipe, chill the punch, and pour from a small serving bowl.

PER SERVING: 62 CALS | 0.6G FAT | TRACE SAT FAT | 7.6G CARBS | 0.7G SUGARS | 2.6G FIBER | 6.8G PROTEIN | TRACE SODIUM

CARROT AND CUCUMBER JUICE

If you don't have romaine lettuce, you can use iceberg instead. You can also use Boston, bibb, or other small butterhead lettuce, but you will need two of them.

SERVES: 1
PREP: 5 MINS COOK: NONE

½ romaine lettuce
2 tomatoes
¾-inch piece of fresh ginger
1 scallion
1 celery stalk, halved
1 carrot, halved
¼ cucumber, plus a slice to garnish (optional)
small handful of ice (optional)

1. Feed the lettuce and tomatoes, then ginger, scallion, celery, carrot, and cucumber, through a juicer.

2. Fill a glass halfway with ice (if using), pour in the juice, add the cucumber slice to garnish (if using), and serve immediately.

KNOW YOUR ONIONS

Onions, leeks, and garlic are rich in antiviral and antibacterial nutrients that are thought to cleanse the system. They are most potent when eaten raw, but use just a little, because they have a strong flavor.

PER SERVING: 144 CALS | 1.5G FAT | 0.1G SAT FAT | 30.8G CARBS | 14.6G SUGARS | 3G FIBER | 7.4G PROTEIN | 120MG SODIUM

SPINACH ENERGY BOOSTER JUICE

*This is a great energy-boosting drink, making it perfect
for breakfast or a midmorning pick-me-up.*

SERVES: 1
PREP: 5 MINS COOK: NONE

2³/4 cups spinach
2 teaspoons acai powder
2 teaspoons manuka honey
¹/8 teaspoon ground cinnamon
1 cup almond milk
crushed ice, to serve (optional)

1. Put the spinach, acai powder, honey, and cinnamon into a blender.

2. Pour the almond milk over the contents in the blender and blend until smooth and creamy.

3. Stir well, pour the juice over the crushed ice, if using, and serve immediately.

NUT ALLERGY
If you have a nut allergy, you can replace
the almond milk with coconut or rice milk instead
for another dairy-free alternative.

PER SERVING: 130 CALS | 6G FAT | 2.2G SAT FAT | 17G CARBS | 12.1G SUGARS | 3G FIBER | 3.1G PROTEIN | 120MG SODIUM

TANTALIZING TOMATO JUICE

For this drink, pick the best-quality tomatoes you can find.
Homegrown or freshly picked ones are perfect, or ones sold on the vine.

SERVES: 1
PREP: 5 MINS   COOK: NONE

2 carrots, halved
1 celery stalk, halved
1-inch slice of broccoli stem
6 basil leaves, plus a sprig to decorate
4 tomatoes
small handful of ice (optional)

1. Feed the carrots, then the celery, broccoli, and the basil, and finally the tomatoes, through a juicer.

2. Fill a glass halfway with ice (if using), then pour in the juice. Garnish with the basil sprig and serve immediately.

HOW TO JUICE HERBS
To get the most juice from herbs, sandwich them between firm fruit or vegetables, so that their weight helps to press down on the leaves as they go through the juicer chute.

PER SERVING: 126 CALS | 1G FAT | 0.1G SAT FAT | 27.5G CARBS | 15.7G SUGARS | 2G FIBER | 5.2G PROTEIN | 120MG SODIUM

LUNCHES

Lemon chicken with zucchini spaghetti	46
Vietnamese shrimp rice rolls	48
Black sesame tofu	50
Chilled green soup	52
Carrot and cashew pâté on crackers	54
South Indian lentil broth	56
Buckwheat noodle salad	58
Energizing arugula soup	60
Baked salmon with sweet potato and cucumber ribbons	62
Baba ghanoush dip with red cabbage salad	64
Green lentils with roasted vegetables	66
Frisée salad with walnut dressing	68
Broiled mackerel with cauliflower couscous	70

LEMON CHICKEN
WITH ZUCCHINI SPAGHETTI

*If you've never tried creating your own "spaghetti" from vegetables,
such as zucchini, you'll love how quick and easy it is and how great it tastes.*

SERVES: 4
PREP: 10 MINS COOK: 8 MINS

4 zucchini, 2 green and 2 yellow
2½ tablespoons olive oil
2 large chicken breasts, cut widthwise into 10 slices
1 teaspoon crushed coriander seeds
1 teaspoon crushed cumin seeds
½ teaspoon sea salt
½ teaspoon pepper
juice of 1 lemon
2 tablespoons toasted pine nuts
3 tablespoons fresh cilantro leaves

1. Using a spiralizer, the side of a box grater, or a vegetable peeler, slice the zucchini into spirals or thin ribbons.

2. Add 1½ teaspoons of the oil to a nonstick skillet and put over high heat. Cook the chicken slices for 1–2 minutes, or until lightly flecked with golden brown, turning once or twice. Turn the heat down to medium and add half of the remaining oil, the seeds, salt, pepper, and half of the lemon juice.

3. Cook, stirring occasionally, for 5 minutes, or until the chicken slices are cooked through. Check that the center of the chicken is no longer pink.

4. Meanwhile, heat the remaining oil in a separate large skillet, add the zucchini spirals ,and sauté for 1–2 minutes, or until just tender and turning golden. Serve the chicken on the zucchini "spaghetti" and sprinkle with the remaining lemon juice, pine nuts, and cilantro leaves.

ZUCCHINI FIBER
Zucchini are a good source of vitamin C and soluble fiber, which may help to relieve irritable bowel symptoms.

PER SERVING: 250 CALS | 14.7G FAT | 2G SAT FAT | 5.3G CARBS | 3G SUGARS | 1.6G FIBER | 24.6G PROTEIN | 360MG SODIUM

VIETNAMESE SHRIMP RICE ROLLS

Wonderfully light and practically fat-free, these delicious snacks are full of protein-rich shellfish and crunchy raw vegetables.

SERVES: 6
PREP: 40 MINS COOK: NONE

1½ ounces vermicelli rice noodles
5½ ounces chilled, prepared jumbo shrimp, rinsed with cold water, drained, and thickly sliced
grated zest of 1 lime
6 sprigs of fresh mint, leaves torn from stems
8 sprigs of fresh cilantro, long stems trimmed
½ cup rinsed and drained bean sprouts
1 carrot, cut into thin strips
¼ cucumber, halved lengthwise, seeded, and cut into thin strips
½ romaine lettuce heart, leaves shredded
6 (8-inch) rice spring roll wrappers

DIPPING SAUCE
juice of 1 lime
1 tablespoon tamari
1 tablespoon packed light brown sugar
1 teaspoon Thai fish sauce
1 red chile, halved, seeded, and finely chopped
2 garlic cloves, finely chopped
1-inch piece fresh ginger, peeled and finely grated

1. Add the noodles to a shallow dish, cover with just-boiled water, then let soften for 5 minutes, or according to the package directions.

2. Mix the shrimp with the lime zest. Arrange the mint, cilantro, bean sprouts, carrot sticks, cucumber sticks, and shredded lettuce in separate piles on a tray. Drain the noodles and transfer to a dish.

3. Pour some just-boiled water into a large, shallow round dish, then dip one of the rice wrappers into the water. Keep moving in the water for 10–15 seconds, or according to the package directions, until soft and transparent, then lift out, drain well, and put onto a cutting board.

4. Arrange a few shrimp in a horizontal line in the center of a rice wrapper, leaving a border of wrapper at each end. Top with some mint leaves and cilantro sprigs, then add a few noodles and bean sprouts. Add some carrot and cucumber, then a little lettuce. Roll up the bottom third of the rice wrapper over the filling, fold in the sides, then roll up tightly to form a log shape. Place on a plate.

5. Repeat with the remaining wrappers until you have 6 rolls.

6. To make the dip, add the lime juice to a small bowl, stir in the tamari, sugar, and fish sauce, then add the chopped chile, garlic, and ginger and stir.

7. Cut each roll in half and serve immediately with individual bowls of the dipping sauce. If planning to serve later, wrap each roll in plastic wrap and chill in the refrigerator for up to 8 hours.

PER SERVING: 112 CALS | 0.4G FAT | TRACE SAT FAT | 22G CARBS | 4.8G SUGARS | 1.4G FIBER | 4.9G PROTEIN | 480MG SODIUM

BLACK SESAME
TOFU

Tofu, made from soybean curd, is a versatile ingredient and works best in flavorful dishes, such as this tasty stir-fry. This makes a wonderful, speedy meal for lunch.

SERVES: 2
PREP: 10 MINS COOK: 15 MINS

1 egg, beaten
1 tablespoon tamari
1½ tablespoons black sesame seeds
9 ounces firm tofu, cut into bite-size chunks
2½ ounces rice noodles
2 tablespoons sesame oil
2 cups small broccoli florets
1 large garlic clove, crushed
1½ teaspoons lemon juice
1 teaspoon crushed red pepper flakes
½ teaspoon pepper
1 teaspoon crushed coriander seeds
1 teaspoon honey
2 scallions, sliced, to garnish
2 tablespoons fresh cilantro leaves, to garnish

1. Combine the beaten egg with half of the tamari in a shallow dish. Put the black sesame seeds into a separate shallow dish. Coat the tofu chunks with the egg mixture and then dip each chunk into the sesame seeds.

2. Cook the noodles according to the package directions. Drain, cover, and set aside.

3. Add half of the sesame oil to a nonstick skillet and put over medium-high heat. Stir-fry the broccoli for 2–3 minutes, then add the garlic, lemon juice, red pepper flakes, pepper, and coriander seeds. Stir for another 1–2 minutes, or until the broccoli is just tender. Stir in the honey, cover the pan, and set aside.

4. Heat the remaining oil in another skillet over medium heat. Add the tofu chunks and sauté them for 3 minutes, turning once or twice. Serve the tofu with the broccoli mixture and noodles and garnish with the sliced scallions and cilantro leaves.

TERRIFIC TOFU
Tofu is cholesterol free and is a good source of protein, iron, calcium, and fiber. It is also quick to cook and ideal in stir-fries, because it readily picks up he flavors you add to the pan.

PER SERVING: 568 CALS | 31G FAT | 4.8G SAT FAT | 49.2G CARBS | 5G SUGARS | 7.9G FIBER | 29.7G PROTEIN | 600MG SODIUM

CHILLED GREEN SOUP

*This simple yet invigorating soup with refreshing cucumber
and plenty of chilled water will cool you down on a hot day.*

SERVES: 2
PREP: 10 MINS COOK: NONE

½ cucumber
2 celery stalks
2 tablespoons chopped fresh parsley,
plus 2 extra sprigs to garnish
2 tablespoons chopped fresh mint
2 tablespoons chopped fresh cilantro
1 cup chilled water

1. Chop the cucumber and celery and add to a blender with
the parsley, mint, cilantro, and water. Blend until smooth.

2. Serve immediately or chill in the refrigerator and stir just
before serving, garnished with parsley.

COOL AS A CUCUMBER
There is some evidence that cucumber can help to
build and maintain healthy connective tissue as we
age. It is a good source of the mineral silica, which
is an essential component of this tissue, as well as of
bone and muscle.

PER SERVING: 25 CALS | 0.2G FAT | TRACE SAT FAT | 4.9G CARBS | 2.3G SUGARS | 1.8G FIBER | 1.2G PROTEIN | 40MG SODIUM

CARROT AND CASHEW PÂTÉ ON CRACKERS

Here is a pâté that is quick to make but has a fresh flavor and a delicious hint of herbs and spices, so it's good enough to serve on a special occasion.

SERVES: 4
PREP: 5 MINS, PLUS SOAKING AND CHILLING   COOK: NONE

1 cup raw cashew nuts
5 carrots, chopped
¼ cup light tahini
juice of 1 lemon
2 teaspoons finely chopped ginger
1 large garlic clove, crushed
½ teaspoon sea salt
2 tablespoons chopped fresh cilantro leaves
1½ cups microgreens, to serve
8 gluten-free mixed seed crackers
(see page 120 or store-bought), to serve

1. Soak the cashew nuts in a large bowl of cold water for at least 4 hours, or overnight, if you have time. Drain thoroughly.

2. Put all of the ingredients, except the fresh cilantro leaves, into an electric food processor or blender. Process until you have a smooth mixture.

3. Stir the cilantro leaves into the mixture and spoon into 3¼-inch round ramekins (individual ceramic dishes). Cover with plastic wrap and chill for 2 hours before serving.

4. Spread the pâté onto the crackers and serve immediately with the microgreens.

CASHEW CRAVINGS
Cashews are high in energy-promoting iron, the antioxidant mineral zinc and nerve-calming magnesium, while sesame seeds have a range of health benefits, including protection from heart disease.

PER SERVING: 453 CALS | 34.3G FAT | 5.1G SAT FAT | 28.5G CARBS | 6.4G SUGARS | 9.6G FIBER | 15.5G PROTEIN | 520MG SODIUM

SOUTH INDIAN LENTIL BROTH

This wonderfully warming soup is great for lunch—
for a more filling dinner, serve with brown rice.

SERVES: 4
PREP: 10 MINS COOK: 30–35 MINS

½ cup yellow lentils (sold as tuvar dal in Indian markets), yellow split peas, or pigeon peas
2½ cups cold water
1 teaspoon ground turmeric
2 tablespoons vegetable or peanut oil
1 teaspoon black mustard seeds
7 fresh curry leaves
1 teaspoon cumin seeds
1 fresh green chile
1 teaspoon tamarind paste
1 teaspoon salt

1. Rinse the lentils or peas under cold water, then put into a saucepan with the water, turmeric, and 1 tablespoon of oil. Cover and simmer for 25–30 minutes, or according to the package directions, until lentils are cooked and tender.

2. Heat the remaining oil in a skillet over medium heat. Add the mustard seeds, curry leaves, cumin seeds, chile, and tamarind paste. When the seeds start to pop, remove the pan from the heat and add to the lentil mixture with the salt.

3. Return the broth to the heat for 2–3 minutes. Ladle into warm bowls and serve immediately.

TASTY TURMERIC

Turmeric comes from a plant native to Indonesia and southern India. The yellow pigment in turmeric has been known to offer protection against inflammatory diseases.

PER SERVING: 163 CALS | 7.7G FAT | 1.2G SAT FAT | 18.7G CARBS | 1.2G SUGARS | 4.3G FIBER | 6G PROTEIN | 600MG SODIUM

BUCKWHEAT NOODLE SALAD

Here is a Japanese-inspired salad made with just-cooked soba noodles, speckled with nutrient-boosting broccoli and protein-packed edamame.

SERVES: 4
PREP: 10 MINS COOK: 10 MINS

5½ ounces soba noodles
1⅓ cups frozen edamame (soybeans)
⅓ head of broccoli, cut into
small florets, stems thinly sliced
1 red bell pepper, halved, seeded, and thinly sliced
1 purple or orange bell pepper,
halved, seeded, and thinly sliced
2 cups thinly sliced cremini mushrooms
¾ cup sunflower seed sprouts

DRESSING
2 tablespoons rice wine vinegar
2 tablespoons tamari
¼ cup rice bran oil
1½-inch piece of fresh ginger,
peeled and finely grated

1. Put some cold water into the bottom half of a steamer, bring to a boil, then add the noodles and frozen edamame and bring back to a boil. Put the broccoli into the top half of the steamer, then put it on the bottom half of the steamer, cover, and steam for 3–5 minutes, or until the noodles and vegetables are just tender. Drain and rinse the noodles and edamame, then drain again and transfer to a salad bowl. Add the broccoli, then let cool.

2. To make the dressing, put the vinegar, tamari, oil, and ginger into a screw–top jar, screw on the lid, and shake well. Drizzle the dressing over the salad and toss gently together.

3. Add the red and purple bell peppers and mushrooms to the salad and toss again. Spoon into four bowls, then top with the sunflower sprouts and serve immediately.

EDAMAME (SOYBEANS)
Fresh soybeans are a good source of all the essential amino acids, making them an excellent bean to eat if you're following a vegetarian diet. They are also a good source of vitamin K, folate, manganese, and fiber.

PER SERVING: 496 CALS | 28.9G FAT | 4.4G SAT FAT | 45G CARBS | 6.6G SUGARS | 9.2G FIBER | 17.8G PROTEIN | 440MG SODIUM

ENERGIZING ARUGULA SOUP

The peppery spice from the arugula and mustard greens is softened by the avocado and coconut milk, creating a creamy but healthy soup.

SERVES: 1
PREP: 10 MINS COOK: NONE

1½ cups arugula,
plus ½ cup extra leaves to garnish
½ cup mustard greens
1 cup chilled water
½ avocado, pitted and flesh scooped from skin
½ cup coconut milk

1. Put the arugula, mustard greens, and water into a blender and blend until smooth.

2. Add the avocado flesh to the blender with the coconut milk and blend until smooth and creamy.

3. Serve immediately or chill in the refrigerator. Stir well just before serving, garnished with a few arugula leaves.

ARUGULA ROUSER
Wild arugula leaves are rich in carotenes and are an excellent source of lutein, which is good for eye health. The indoles in arugula are also linked to protection from colon cancer.

PER SERVING: 379 CALS | 37.9G FAT | 25.2G SAT FAT | 11.9G CARBS | 4.4G SUGARS | 6.1G FIBER | 5.4G PROTEIN | TRACE SODIUM

BAKED SALMON WITH SWEET POTATO AND CUCUMBER RIBBONS

*A simple and refreshing lunch that is packed with nutrition,
because it contains vitamins C and E as well as essential omega-3 fatty acids.*

SERVES: 4
PREP: 15 MINS   COOK: 16 MINS

2 sweet potatoes
1½ tablespoons extra virgin canola oil
½ teaspoon sea salt
½ teaspoon pepper
1 cucumber, trimmed
1 tablespoon white wine vinegar
1 teaspoon mild-flavored honey, such as acacia
4 thick salmon fillets, about 4½ ounces each
2 teaspoons crushed cumin seeds
1 tablespoon chopped fresh dill, to garnish

1. Preheat the oven to 375°F. Slice the sweet potatoes lengthwise into long, thin ribbons, using a vegetable peeler, the side of a box grater, or a spiralizer. Toss the ribbons in a bowl with half of the oil and half of the salt and pepper, then arrange in a baking pan. Place the pan near the top of the preheated oven and cook for 6 minutes. Leave the oven on.

2. Meanwhile, slice the cucumber into long, thin ribbons, using a vegetable peeler, the side of a box grater, or a spiralizer. Place the ribbons in a bowl. Mix together the vinegar and honey in a small bowl, then sprinkle the dressing over the cucumber ribbons and stir gently to combine.

3. Put the salmon fillets in a baking pan, brush with the remaining oil, sprinkle with the crushed cumin seeds and the rest of the salt and pepper, and place the pan in the center of the oven. At the same time, use tongs to turn the sweet potato ribbons over and return them to the oven.

4. Bake for an additional 10 minutes, or until the salmon is cooked through and the potato ribbons are tender and turning golden. If the potatoes need another minute or two, remove the salmon from the oven and let stand while the potatoes finish cooking.

5. Serve the salmon with the potato ribbons and the dressed cucumber ribbons on the side. Garnish with the chopped dill.

PER SERVING: 340 CALS | 18.9G FAT | 1.6G SAT FAT | 26.7G CARBS | 7.7G SUGARS | 3.8G FIBER | 27.4G PROTEIN | 400MG SODIUM

BABA GHANOUSH DIP
WITH RED CABBAGE SALAD

Broiling eggplants until blackened all over
gives this dip a wonderfully smoky flavor.

SERVES: 4
PREP: 10 MINS COOK: 20 MINS

2 carrots
3³/₄ cups shredded red cabbage
¹/₃ cup raisins
4¹/₂ cups mixed salad greens, such as a mixture of red-stemmed baby Swiss chard and mache
juice of 1 orange
¹/₂ teaspoon pepper

DIP
3 eggplants
3 garlic cloves, finely chopped
2 tablespoons tahini
3 tablespoons hemp oil
pepper (optional)

1. To make the dip, preheat the broiler to high and remove the broiler rack. Prick both ends of each eggplant with a fork, put them in the broiler pan and broil 2 inches away from the heat source, turning several times, for 15–20 minutes, or until blackened. Let cool.

2. Shave the carrots into long, thin ribbons, using a swivel-blade vegetable peeler, then put them onto a serving plate. Add the cabbage, then sprinkle with the raisins and salad greens. Drizzle with the orange juice and season with the pepper.

3. Cut the eggplants in half and scoop the soft flesh away from the blackened skins, using a tablespoon. Finely chop the flesh, then put it into a bowl. Add the garlic, tahini, and hemp oil, season with a little pepper, if using, and mix. Spoon into a serving bowl and nestle in the center of the salad. Let the diners spoon the dip over the salad to taste.

RED CABBAGE FOR DETOX
With its intense deep-purple color, red cabbage has a strong concentration of flavonoids —these are antioxidants that have been linked to cancer protection.

PER SERVING: 309 CALS | 8.4G FAT | 0.9G SAT FAT | 43.6G CARBS | 25.6G SUGARS | 13.5G FIBER | 7G PROTEIN | 120MG SODIUM

GREEN LENTILS
WITH ROASTED VEGETABLES

Lentils and whole grains are vital in any detox diet. Rich in complex carbs, fiber, protein, vitamins, and minerals, they make a filling base to any meal.

SERVES: 4
PREP: 15 MINS COOK: 30 MINS

2 small red bell peppers, quartered and seeded
2 zucchini, thickly sliced
2 red onions, each cut into 8 wedges
4 tomatoes, halved
10½ ounces baby eggplants, halved lengthwise
3 stems of fresh thyme, leaves picked
2 garlic cloves, finely chopped
½ teaspoon pepper
3 tablespoons olive oil
1 cup green lentils
½ cup coarsely chopped fresh flat–leaf parsley, to garnish

DRESSING
3 tablespoons hemp oil
2 tablespoons balsamic vinegar
juice of 1 lemon
pepper (optional)

1. Preheat the oven to 400°F. Arrange the bell peppers, skin side up, in a large roasting pan. Add the zucchini, onions, tomatoes, and eggplants, and arrange in a single layer.

2. Sprinkle the thyme and garlic over the vegetables. Season with the pepper and drizzle with the olive oil. Roast for 30 minutes, or until the vegetables are softened and browned around the edges.

3. Put the lentils into a saucepan of boiling water. Bring back to a boil, then simmer for 20 minutes, or according to the package directions, until just tender. Drain into a strainer, rinse with cold water, then drain again. Transfer to a salad bowl and let cool.

4. To make the dressing, put the hemp oil, balsamic vinegar, and lemon juice into a screw–top jar and season with pepper, if using. Screw on the lid and shake well.

5. Drizzle the dressing over the lentils and toss gently together. Peel the skins away from the bell peppers and cut into slices, then add them to the salad. Add the remaining roasted vegetables and any pan juices, then garnish with the parsley and serve.

HOLD THE SALT
On a detox, you should cut right down on salt. Take the salt shaker from the table and gradually cut down on the amount you use in cooking. Add spices, herbs, garlic, and vinegars instead.

PER SERVING: 476 CALS | 15G FAT | 1.8G SAT FAT | 57.2G CARBS | 13.6G SUGARS | 12.3G FIBER | 17.4G PROTEIN | TRACE SODIUM

FRISÉE SALAD WITH WALNUT DRESSING

This simple yet flavor-packed salad is wonderful and light, with crispy leaves and honey-toasted walnuts.

SERVES: 4
PREP: 10 MINS COOK: 5 MINS, PLUS COOLING

½ frisée lettuce, leaves separated
and torn into bite-size pieces
1 romaine lettuce heart, leaves separated
and torn into bite-size pieces

DRESSING
½ cup walnut pieces, larger pieces broken up
3 tablespoons olive oil
1 teaspoon honey
1 tablespoon white wine vinegar
1 teaspoon gluten-free Dijon mustard
¼ teaspoon pepper

1. To make the dressing, put the walnuts into a skillet, add 1 tablespoon of the oil, and cook over medium heat for 2–3 minutes, or until lightly toasted. Remove from the heat, drizzle with the honey, and stir. The heat from the pan will be enough to caramelize the mixture slightly.

2. Add the remaining oil, stir, then let cool for 15 minutes so the walnuts flavor the oil. When it is cool, put the vinegar and mustard into a small bowl, season with the pepper, and beat together. Stir this into the walnuts and oil.

3. Put both torn lettuce into a salad bowl. Spoon the walnut dressing over the leaves, toss gently together, and serve.

WALNUT WONDER
Walnuts contain mostly polyunsaturated fatty acids. They are also rich in protein and fiber, and they provide many of the essential amino acids.

PER SERVING: 224 CALS | 19.7G FAT | 2.3G SAT FAT | 10.8G CARBS | 3.8G SUGARS | 6.3G FIBER | 4.9G PROTEIN | 40MG SODIUM

BROILED MACKEREL WITH CAULIFLOWER COUSCOUS

You won't miss standard grain couscous once you've tried the cauliflower version —it really is gorgeous, tasty, and light. The herbs and spices give a zesty finish that goes well with oily fish.

SERVES: 4
PREP: 15 MINS COOK: 6 MINS

CAULIFLOWER COUSCOUS
1 head of cauliflower
1 tablespoon extra virgin olive oil
zest and juice of 1 lime
1 red chile, seeded and finely chopped
4 scallions, chopped
1 garlic clove, minced
1/3 cup chopped fresh flat-leaf parsley
1/4 cup chopped fresh mint leaves
1/2 teaspoon sea salt
1/2 teaspoon black pepper

MACKEREL
4 skin-on mackerel fillets, about 4 1/2 ounces each
1 tablespoon extra virgin olive oil
1 teaspoon sweet smoked paprika
1 lime, quartered

1. Line a broiler pan with aluminum foil and preheat the broiler to high.

2. Grate the cauliflower into a large bowl (discarding the core in the center) or cut it into small florets, then pulse in a food processor for a few seconds until you have couscouslike "grains." Add the oil, lime zest and juice, chile, scallions, garlic, herbs, salt, and pepper. Mix thoroughly to combine.

3. Make three cuts across the skin sides of the fish with a sharp knife and rub in the oil and paprika. Broil in the preheated broiler for 5 minutes, skin side up, or until crisp, then turn over with a spatula and cook for an additional minute.

4. Divide the cauliflower couscous among serving plates and top with the mackerel. Serve immediately with the lime wedges.

MIGHTY MACKEREL
Mackerel is high in healthy omega-3 fats, with about 2.6g in a small 3 1/2-ounce serving— researchers often recommend consuming 1–2g of omega-3 fats a day.

PER SERVING: 369 CALS | 24.6G FAT | 5.1G SAT FAT | 11.4G CARBS | 3.7G SUGARS | 3.8G FIBER | 26.6G PROTEIN | 440MG SODIUM

MAIN DISHES

RAW VEGETABLE LASAGNA

There are several elements to this wonderful raw vegan lasagna,
but it is easy to put together and is ideal for a dinner party.

SERVES: 2
PREP: 1 HOUR 30 MINS   COOK: NONE

1 zucchini, thinly sliced lengthwise
1¹/₂ teaspoons olive oil
2 teaspoons balsamic vinegar
¹/₄ teaspoon salt

NUT CHEESE LAYER
²/₃ cup shelled macadamia nuts
¹/₂ small yellow bell pepper, diced
1 tablespoon nutritional yeast flakes
1¹/₂ tablespoons lemon juice
¹/₄ teaspoon salt

TOMATO SAUCE
2 tablespoons tomato paste
¹/₂ teaspoon garlic paste
¹/₄ teaspoon smoked paprika
¹/₂ teaspoon salt (optional)

AVOCADO PESTO
¹/₃ cup pine nuts
1 large ripe avocado, coarsely chopped
3 tablespoons fresh basil leaves
1 small garlic clove, crushed
juice of ¹/₂ lime
¹/₄ teaspoon salt

2 large tomatoes
1 cup baby spinach leaves
2 teaspoons each pine nuts and basil leaves, to garnish

1. To make the zucchini layer, place the zucchini in a dish that will hold the slices in one layer. Cover the slices with the oil, vinegar, and salt, making sure that each slice is well covered, then set aside for up to 1 hour to soften and absorb the flavors.

2. To make the cheese layer, pulse all the ingredients in a blender until you have a smooth, light paste.

3. To make the tomato sauce, combine all the ingredients in a small bowl, then add about 2 tablespoons of cold water and mix thoroughly. Add a little more water until you have a pouring consistency. Add salt, if using.

4. To make the avocado pesto layer, put the pine nuts into an electric mini chopper or blender and process for a few seconds, or until chopped but not pureed. Add the avocado chunks, basil leaves, garlic, lime juice, and salt and pulse until you have a lightly textured mixture. Slice the tomatoes so that you have six inside slices from each. Discard the outer slices.

5. Layer the two lasagne directly onto plates. Arrange one-quarter of the zucchini slices in a rectangle on the center of each plate. For each plate, top with on 3-quarter of the spinach leaves, then spoon one-quarter of the nut cheese over them. Add one-quarter of the tomato slices and top them with one-quarter of the avocado pesto. For each plate, add another one-quarter of the tomato slices, one-quarter of the cheese, one-quarter of the spinach, and one-quarter of the avocado pesto. Finish by placing the remaining zucchini slices on top of each lasagna.

6. Toast the pine nuts in a dry skillet. Drizzle the sauce over the two lasagne and garnish with toasted pine nuts and basil leaves.

PER SERVING: 799 CALS | 72.6G FAT | 9.9G SAT FAT | 37.8G CARBS | 14.1G SUGARS | 16.5G FIBER | 15.1G PROTEIN | 920MG SODIUM

STEAMED MUSSELS IN LEMONGRASS BROTH

*The clean, refreshing flavor of lemongrass is perfect
with the richly flavored mussels in this filling broth.*

SERVES: 4
PREP: 10 MINS COOK: 20 MINS

2 shallots, chopped
2 lemongrass stalks, fibrous outer leaves
discarded, stems bashed with the flat of a knife
4 thin slices galangal or fresh ginger
2 garlic cloves, chopped
1 small tomato, chopped
1¼ cups gluten-free fish broth
2 pounds fresh mussels, scrubbed and debearded
3 tablespoons butter
2 tablespoons chopped fresh cilantro, to garnish
salt and pepper, to taste (optional)

1. Put the shallots, lemongrass, galangal, garlic, and tomato into a large, covered wok. Pour in the broth, season with salt and pepper, if using, and bring to a boil. Reduce the heat slightly and simmer for 5 minutes.

2. Discard any mussels with broken shells and any that refuse to close when tapped. Add the mussels to the wok, cover, and cook for 5 minutes, shaking the wok occasionally, until the mussel shells have opened. Discard any mussels that remain closed.

3. Drain the mussels in a colander set over a bowl. Strain the liquid, using a strainer, into a small wok. Simmer over low heat for a few minutes, then whisk in the butter. Taste and adjust the seasoning, if necessary.

4. Divide the mussels among warm bowls. Pour the liquid over them, garnish with the cilantro, and serve immediately.

MUSSEL POWER
Mussels are low in saturated fat and high in protein, while also containing some omega-3 essential fats and a wide range of vitamins and minerals in good amounts. They are also low in dietary cholesterol.

PER SERVING: 142 CALS | 9.8G FAT | 5.7G SAT FAT | 6.5G CARBS | 1.1G SUGARS | 0.6G FIBER | 7.6G PROTEIN | 560MG SODIUM

CREOLE CHICKEN WITH PARSNIP RICE

Creole dishes are full of vegetables and strong on flavor and color, so they are sure to please around the dinner table. This tasty take on Chicken Creole is low in calories but packed with nutrients.

SERVES: 4
PREP: 15 MINS COOK: 30 MINS

2 tablespoons extra virgin canola oil
4 small chicken breasts, each sliced into 3 pieces
1 large onion, sliced
2 celery stalks, finely chopped
1 green bell pepper, seeded and thinly sliced
1 yellow bell pepper, seeded and thinly sliced
2 garlic cloves, crushed
1 teaspoon smoked paprika
1¼ cups canned diced tomatoes
1 teaspoon sea salt
1 teaspoon pepper
2 large parsnips, coarsely chopped
1 tablespoon hemp seeds
¼ cup fresh cilantro leaves, plus a sprig to garnish

1. Heat half of the oil in a large skillet over high heat. Add the sliced chicken pieces and cook for 2 minutes, or until lightly browned. Remove the chicken pieces from the pan with a slotted spatula and transfer to a plate. Set aside.

2. Add the onion, celery, and bell peppers to the skillet with half of the remaining oil. Turn the heat down to medium and cook, stirring frequently, for about 10 minutes, or until the vegetables have softened and are just turning golden.

3. Stir in the garlic and paprika and cook for 30 seconds. Add the diced tomatoes and half of the salt and pepper. Return the chicken to the pan, bring to a simmer, and cook for 10 minutes.

4. Meanwhile, add the parsnips to the bowl of a food processor. Process on high until they resemble rice grains, then stir in the hemp seeds and the remaining salt and pepper.

5. Heat the remaining oil in a skillet over medium heat. Stir in the parsnip rice and sauté for 2 minutes, then stir through the cilantro leaves. Serve the chicken mixture spooned over the parsnip rice and garnished with the cilantro sprig.

PARSNIP POWER
Parsnips are rich in soluble fiber, which can help prevent diabetes and high blood cholesterol.

PER SERVING: 339 CALS | 12.2G FAT | 1.3G SAT FAT | 25G CARBS | 10.1G SUGARS | 6.6G FIBER | 32.2G PROTEIN | 780MG SODIUM

QUINOA PIZZA
WITH CASHEW CHEESE

Generously topped with Mediterranean vegetables, this pizza also features a delicious, nutty high-protein quinoa crust and a perfect finishing touch in tangy cashew cheese.

SERVES: 2
PREP: 30 MINS, PLUS OVERNIGHT SOAKING
COOK: 20 MINS

CASHEW CHEESE
½ cup raw cashew nuts, soaked overnight in water
1 small garlic clove, crushed
1 tablespoon nutritional yeast flakes
1½ teaspoons lemon juice

TOPPING
½ cup drained sun-dried tomatoes in oil
3 tablespoons tomato puree or tomato sauce
1 garlic clove, crushed
½ teaspoon salt (optional)
½ red bell pepper, seeded and sliced
½ green bell pepper, seeded and sliced
1 small red onion, cut into 6 wedges
2 teaspoons dried mixed herbs
5 pieces grilled artichoke heart in oil, drained
1 tomato, coarsely chopped

QUINOA BASE
¾ cup white quinoa (soaked in 2 cups water for about 8 hours)
½ teaspoon gluten-free baking powder
½ teaspoon salt
2½ tablespoons olive oil, plus 1 teaspoon for brushing

1. To make the cashew cheese, drain the cashew nuts and add to an electric food processor or blender with the garlic and 3 tablespoons of water. Process until smooth. Stir in the nutritional yeast flakes and lemon juice and process for a few more seconds. For the pizza, you want a "dropping consistency" texture, not quite as firm as hummus, so add a little extra water, if necessary, and blend again. Spoon the cheese out and set aside.

2. Preheat the oven to 375°F. Line a 9-inch shallow cake pan with parchment paper and grease the paper with 1 teaspoon of oil.

3. To make a tomato paste, blend the sun-dried tomatoes with the tomato puree or sauce and garlic. Add salt, if using, and stir in a little water for a spreading consistency, if needed.

4. To make the quinoa crust, drain the water from the quinoa and put into a blender with the baking powder, salt, ¼ cup of water, and 2 tablespoons of the olive oil. Blend until you have a thick, creamy batter. Pour into the prepared cake pan and shape into a circle. Bake in the preheated oven for 15 minutes, or until the top is golden. Remove from the pan and transfer to a wire rack to cool.

5. Meanwhile, toss the bell peppers, onion, and mixed herbs with the remaining half a tablespoon of oil and roast in a baking pan in the preheated oven for 10–15 minutes, or until softened and turning lightly golden. Remove from the heat and set aside. Spread the tomato paste over the pizza crust, leaving the edges clear. Arrange the bell peppers, onion, artichoke pieces, and chopped tomato on the pizza and then drop dollops of the cashew cheese over the top. Return to the oven for 5 minutes, or until the vegetables are hot and the cashew cheese is tinged golden and set.

PER SERVING: 759 CALS | 44G FAT | 6.8G SAT FAT | 76.2G CARBS | 10.7G SUGARS | 14.1G FIBER | 21.4G PROTEIN | 1,040MG SODIUM

VIETNAMESE VEGETABLE SOUP

*This wonderful soup is laden with vegetables and noodles,
making it a flavor-packed and filling choice for dinner.*

SERVES: 4
PREP: 10 MINS COOK: 30 MINS

6½ cups gluten-free reduced-sodium
vegetable broth
2 tablespoons tamari
2 garlic cloves, thinly sliced
1-inch piece ginger, peeled and thinly sliced
1 cinnamon stick
1 bay leaf
1 carrot, cut into thin batons
1 small fennel bulb, thinly sliced
5½ ounces vermicelli rice noodles
1¼ cups sliced white button mushrooms
1 cup bean sprouts
4 scallions, thinly sliced diagonally
3 tablespoons chopped fresh cilantro
fresh basil leaves, chopped red chiles,
lime wedges, and tamari, to serve (optional)

1. Put the broth into a large saucepan with the tamari, garlic, ginger, cinnamon, and bay leaf. Bring to a boil, reduce the heat, cover, and simmer for about 20 minutes.

2. Add the carrot and fennel and simmer for 1 minute. Add the noodles and simmer for an additional 4 minutes.

3. Add the mushrooms, bean sprouts, and scallions and return to a boil.

4. Ladle into warm soup bowls and sprinkle with the cilantro. Remove and discard the bay leaf and cinnamon. Serve immediately with basil leaves, chiles, lime wedges, and tamari, if using.

GREAT BEAN SPROUTS
Bean sprouts are ideal for losing weight,
because they are low in calories and high in fiber.
They are also a good source of vitamin B.

PER SERVING: 205 CALS | 1.6G FAT | 0.8G SAT FAT | 42.3G CARBS | 5.8G SUGARS | 3.7G FIBER | 5.8G PROTEIN | 1,400MG SODIUM

TAMARIND TURKEY WITH ZUCCHINI NOODLES

Detoxing doesn't mean losing the flavor in your food, as this delicious Thai dish will prove. This recipe is rich with health-giving galangal, garlic, and chile.

SERVES: 4
PREP: 15 MINS, PLUS STANDING   COOK: 10 MINS

1 pound 2 ounces turkey breast, diced
1½ tablespoons tamari
3 zucchini
1½ tablespoons peanut oil
3 ounces small okra
1-inch piece fresh galangal or ginger, peeled and grated
3 garlic cloves, crushed
1 large red chile, finely chopped
1 lemongrass stalk, bashed
2 tablespoons rice wine

TAMARIND SAUCE
1 tablespoon tamarind paste
½ cup gluten-free chicken broth
2 teaspoons Thai fish sauce
1 tablespoon raw palm sugar or brown sugar
1 teaspoon cornstarch

1. Toss the turkey pieces with 1 tablespoon of the tamari to coat. Let marinate for 5 minutes.

2. Meanwhile, make the tamarind sauce by combining all the ingredients thoroughly in a small bowl. Slice the zucchini into thin ribbons, using a spiralizer, the side of a box grater, or a vegetable peeler.

3. Add half of the oil to a large skillet and put over medium-high heat. Add the coated turkey pieces and stir-fry for 3 minutes, or until cooked through. Remove the turkey with a slotted spoon to a warm plate. Turn the heat down to medium.

4. Add the okra to the pan with the remaining oil and stir-fry for 2 minutes, stirring from time to time. Add the galangal, garlic, chile, lemongrass, rice wine, and remaining tamari and stir for an additional 2 minutes. Return the turkey pieces to the pan and add the tamarind sauce. Stir well to combine and simmer for 3 minutes. Add a little extra chicken broth or water if the sauce gets too thick.

5. While the sauce is simmering, steam the zucchini noodles over a saucepan of boiling water for 30 seconds, until softened and warm. Remove the lemongrass stalk from the turkey mixture and serve immediately, with the noodles on the side.

PER SERVING: 270 CALS | 8G FAT | 1.4G SAT FAT | 15.4G CARBS | 7.7G SUGARS | 2.3G FIBER | 32.2G PROTEIN | 600MG SODIUM

BROILED CAULIFLOWER CUTLETS WITH KALE SLAW

Once you have tried broiled cauliflower "cutlets," you will never want to eat it any other way—they really are delicious, especially served with vitamin-rich kale slaw.

SERVES: 4
PREP: 20 MINS, PLUS STANDING   COOK: 15 MINS

KALE SLAW
2 cups shredded tender kale leaves
2 carrots, shredded
1 small red onion, thinly sliced
2 tablespoons extra virgin canola oil
1 teaspoon Dijon mustard
1½ teaspoons apple cider vinegar
2 teaspoons maple syrup
sea salt and pepper (optional)
1 tablespoon pumpkin seeds
1 tablespoon sunflower seeds

CAULIFLOWER CUTLETS
2 heads of cauliflower
3 tablespoons extra virgin canola oil
juice of ½ lime
1 teaspoon sweet paprika
1 large garlic clove, crushed
½ teaspoon sea salt
½ teaspoon pepper

1. In a serving bowl, combine the kale, carrot, and onion. In a small bowl, thoroughly mix together the oil, mustard, vinegar, maple syrup, and salt and pepper, if using, and stir into the slaw. Cover and set aside to rest for up to 1 hour. Before serving, sprinkle the seeds over the slaw.

2. Preheat the broiler to medium–hot. Meanwhile, remove the leaves from the cauliflower and cut the stem across the bottom so it will sit firmly on your cutting board. Using a sharp knife, cut vertically down about 2 inches through the first cauliflower. Remove the florets that fall and repeat on the other side so you are left with the firm centered piece of the vegetable. Now slice through the cauliflower and stem to produce "cutlets" that are ¾–1 inch thick. You should get two cutlets from each cauliflower.

3. Cover the rack of a large broiler pan with aluminium foil and place the cutlets on top. Combine the oil, lime juice, paprika, garlic, salt, and pepper in a small bowl and brush the cutlets all over with this mixture. Broil the cutlets about 2 inches from the heat source for 8 minutes, or until the cutlets are slightly browned.

4. Turn the cutlets over carefully with a large metal spatula and brush again with any remaining oil mixture and any juices that have collected on the foil. Broil for an additional 6 minutes, or until the cutlets are browned and just tender when pierced with a sharp knife. Serve immediately with the kale slaw.

PER SERVING: 296 CALS | 21.1G FAT | 1.9G SAT FAT | 24.5G CARBS | 10.1G SUGARS | 8.1G FIBER | 8.1G PROTEIN | 400MG SODIUM

TOFU AND MISO SALAD

Protein-rich tofu cooked in a tamari, miso, and garlic glaze and served with a crispy, crunchy asparagus and bean sprout salad is both superhealthy and superb!

SERVES: 4

PREP: 15 MINS COOK: 10 MINS

14 ounces firm tofu, drained and cut into ½-inch slices
1 tablespoon sesame seeds
1 cup thinly sliced snow peas
1 cup bean sprouts
16 asparagus spears, trimmed and cut into long, thin slices
1 zucchini, cut into matchsticks
1 Boston, bibb, or other small butterhead lettuce, leaves separated and cut into long slices
½ cup coarsely chopped fresh cilantro
2½ cups mixed seed sprouts, such as alfalfa and radish sprouts

DRESSING

3 tablespoons rice wine vinegar
2 tablespoons tamari
3 tablespoons sunflower oil
1 tablespoon sweet white miso
2 garlic cloves

1. To make the dressing, put the vinegar and tamari into a screw-top jar, then add the oil, miso, and garlic. Screw on the lid and shake well.

2. Preheat the broiler to high and line the broiler pan with aluminum foil. Put the tofu on the foil in a single layer. Mark crisscross lines over each slice, using a knife, then sprinkle with the sesame seeds. Spoon half the dressing over the top, then broil for 8–10 minutes, turning once, until browned.

3. Put the snow peas, bean sprouts, asparagus, zucchini, and lettuce onto a platter. Pour over the remaining dressing and toss gently together. Sprinkle with the cilantro and sprouts, then top with the hot tofu. Drizzle with any pan juices and serve immediately.

MISO MAGIC
Miso is associated with good digestive health, because it feeds the beneficial probiotic bacteria present in the body. This supports the absorption of nutrients to keep you feeling healthy.

PER SERVING: 316 CALS | 20.9G FAT | 2.5G SAT FAT | 16G CARBS | 6.3G SUGARS | 6.2G FIBER | 22G PROTEIN | 560MG SODIUM

MONKFISH AND BABY BROCCOLI COCONUT CURRY

Fish, coconut, and spices were simply made for each other,
as you'll know if you try this quick-and-simple curry for dinner.

SERVES: 4
PREP: 15 MINS COOK: 20 MINS

1 large onion, chopped
2 teaspoons Thai fish sauce
juice of ½ lime
2 red chiles, 1 trimmed and 1 chopped
1 green chile, trimmed
2 teaspoons crushed coriander seeds
2 teaspoons crushed cumin seeds
1-inch piece fresh ginger, chopped
3 garlic cloves, coarsely chopped
½ lemongrass stalk
1½ tablespoons peanut oil
5 curry leaves
1¼ cups coconut milk
12 ounces baby broccoli,
each spear cut in two
1 pound 2 ounces monkfish fillet, cubed

1. Add the onion, fish sauce, lime juice, trimmed chiles, seeds, ginger, garlic, lemongrass, and half of the oil to the bowl of a blender or food processor and process until you have a paste. Put the mixture into a skillet and cook over medium heat for 2 minutes. Stir in the curry leaves and coconut milk and simmer for an additional 10 minutes.

2. Meanwhile, add the remaining oil to another skillet and put over high heat. Stir–fry the broccoli for 2 minutes, or until just tender. Set aside.

3. Add the monkfish cubes to the curry pan and bring back to a simmer. Cook for 2 minutes, then add the broccoli spears to the pan and continue cooking for an additional minute. Serve the curry with the remaining chopped chile sprinkled over the top.

BOUNTIFUL BROCCOLI
Baby broccoli is high in the plant chemical sulforaphane, which is thought to help prevent cancer, as well as being rich in vitamin C, iron, and fiber.

PER SERVING: 346 CALS | 21.5G FAT | 12.8G SAT FAT | 17.3G CARBS | 6.8G SUGARS | 4G FIBER | 22.8G PROTEIN | 80MG SODIUM

PEA AND SEED SPROUT BUCKWHEAT POWER BOWL

Seed and bean sprouts make a wonderful addition to a healthy salad at any time of year, while buckwheat adds fiber and a superb nutty flavor.

SERVES: 4
PREP: 10 MINS, PLUS COOLING   COOK: 20 MINS

4 carrots, cut into quarters lengthwise
2½ tablespoons extra virgin canola oil
1½ tablespoons maple syrup
⅔ cup roasted buckwheat groats (kasha)
4 cups mixed seed sprouts (such as adzuki beans, alfalfa, radish, and lentil)
¼ cucumber, diced
2 celery stalks, diced
1 red-skinned apple, diced
4 scallions, diced
½ cup cooked small peas
juice of 1 orange
juice of ½ lemon
½ teaspoon sea salt
½ teaspoon pepper
1 cup pea shoots

1. Preheat the oven to 375°F.

2. Toss the carrots in 1½ teaspoons of the oil and in 1½ teaspoons of the maple syrup. Roast in the preheated oven for 20 minutes, or until golden and just tender. Let cool.

3. Meanwhile, pour the groats into ¾ cup of boiling water in a large saucepan. Stir and bring to a boil, then reduce to a simmer, cover, and cook for 10 minutes, or according to the package directions, or until the groats are cooked. Turn the heat off and let the pan stand on the heat for a few minutes with the lid on, then put into a serving bowl and let cool.

4. Mix the cooled groats with the seed sprouts, cucumber, celery, apple, scallions, and peas.

5. Combine the remaining canola oil and maple syrup with the orange and lemon juices and salt and pepper in a small bowl. Stir this dressing into the buckwheat mixture. Top with the roasted carrots and pea shoots, then serve in individual bowls.

SUPER SPROUTS
Seed sprouts and bean sprouts contain digestive enzymes—most are rich in antioxidants and are a great source of vitamin C.

PER SERVING: 300 CALS | 10.1G FAT | 0.8G SAT FAT | 49.3G CARBS | 15.8G SUGARS | 10.5G FIBER | 9G PROTEIN | 360MG SODIUM

CAULIFLOWER AND LIMA BEAN STEW

This is a hearty and colorful one-pot dish that needs no accompanying carbs, because the lima beans contain a good balance of both protein and starch.

SERVES: 4
PREP: 10 MINS COOK: 35 MINS

2 tablespoons olive oil
2 large red onions, sliced
2 carrots, cut into ¾-inch dice
2 celery stalks, cut into ¾-inch dice
3 garlic cloves, crushed
1 (14½-ounce) can plum tomatoes in juice
1 cup gluten-free vegetable broth
1 tablespoon tomato paste
1½ teaspoons dried mixed herbs
½ teaspoon pepper
salt (optional)
2 (15-ounce) cans lima beans, drained and rinsed
1 head of cauliflower, divided into florets
1 teaspoon sweet paprika

1. Add the oil to a large lidded saucepan and put over medium-hot heat. Add the onions, carrots, and celery and cook for 5 minutes, or until lightly browned, stirring from time to time. Stir in the garlic and cook for a minute.

2. Add the canned tomatoes, coarsely crushing any whole ones against the sides of the pan, and their juice. Stir in the broth, tomato paste, herbs, pepper, and salt, if using. Bring to a simmer, reduce the heat to low, and cover with the lid. Cook for 20 minutes, or until the vegetables are all tender.

3. Stir in the lima beans and cook for an additional 5 minutes. Place the cauliflower florets on top of the stew, put the lid back on, and simmer for an additional 5 minutes, or until the cauliflower is just tender when the stems are pierced with a sharp knife.

4. Serve the stew immediately, garnished with the sweet paprika.

ROMANESCO RULES
You can also make this stew with romanesco if you grow it or find it at a farmer's market. Romanesco is an attractive type of brassica that is closely related to both broccoli and cauliflower and has similar nutritional benefits.

PER SERVING: 301 CALS | 9.8G FAT | 1.6G SAT FAT | 39.2G CARBS | 11.3G SUGARS | 12.9G FIBER | 13G PROTEIN | 320MG SODIUM

INDONESIAN MIXED VEGETABLE SALAD

Tossing raw cauliflower and broccoli with crunchy bean sprouts and cucumber and coating them with an Indonesian dressing turns everyday ingredients into something special.

SERVES: 4
PREP: 10 MINS COOK: 5 MINS, PLUS COOLING

½ small head of cauliflower,
cored and cut into small florets
¼ head of broccoli, destemmed
and cut into small florets
2 cups shredded savoy cabbage
1½ cups bean sprouts
1 cucumber, peeled, halved lengthwise, seeded, and
thickly sliced
1 red bell pepper, halved,
seeded, and finely chopped

DRESSING

2 tablespoons peanut oil
½ cup finely chopped unsalted peanuts
2 garlic cloves, finely chopped
2 tablespoons tamari
juice of 2 limes
½ red chile, seeded and finely chopped

1. Put the cauliflower, broccoli, cabbage, bean sprouts, cucumber, and red bell pepper into a salad bowl and toss together gently.

2. To make the dressing, heat 1 tablespoon of the oil in a skillet over medium heat. Add the peanuts and garlic and stir-fry for 2–3 minutes, or until lightly browned. Remove from the heat and stir in the tamari, lime juice, chile, and remaining oil. Let cool.

3. When ready to eat, spoon the dressing over the salad and toss together gently. Spoon into four bowls, then serve immediately.

BEAN SPROUT BONANZA
Bean sprouts are low in calories
and can be added to salads and Asian dishes
in place of rice or noodles.

PER SERVING: 259 CALS | 17.8G FAT | 2.6G SAT FAT | 20.4G CARBS | 8.2G SUGARS | 6.6G FIBER | 10.8G PROTEIN | 480MG SODIUM

ROASTED FENNEL AND ARTICHOKE WITH CARAWAY DRESSING

Here is an aromatic warm salad ideal for keeping hunger at bay—although the dish is low in calories, its high fiber content will keep hunger pangs away for several hours.

SERVES: 4
PREP: 10 MINS COOK: 25 MINS

2 large fennel bulbs
1 large red bell pepper, cut into 12 slices
13–14 artichoke hearts in olive oil, drained,
and 2 tablespoons of the oil reserved
½ teaspoon sea salt
½ teaspoon pepper
1 tablespoon white wine vinegar
1½ teaspoons caraway seeds, lightly crushed
1 teaspoon honey
1 teaspoon sweet paprika

1. Trim the fennel bulbs of any leaves and reserve them. Slice the fennel into thick slices widthwise. Preheat the oven to 375°F.

2. Brush the fennel and bell pepper slices with ½ tablespoon of the reserved artichoke oil. Season with a pinch of the sea salt and pepper and roast in the preheated oven for 25 minutes, or until browned (the bell peppers may need to come out before the fennel). Turn over halfway through.

3. Meanwhile, to make a dressing, combine the remaining 1½ tablespoons of artichoke heart oil with the wine vinegar, caraway seeds, honey, half of the paprika, and the remaining salt and pepper. Cut the artichoke hearts in half if they are not already cut.

4. Arrange the fennel and bell pepper slices on serving dishes with the artichokes. Drizzle with the dressing and serve garnished with the reserved fennel leaves and the remaining paprika.

FANTASTIC FENNEL
Fennel contains several valuable plant chemicals, including rutin, quercetin, and kaempferol, that have strong antioxidant effects, as well as the anti-inflammatory anethole.

PER SERVING: 128 CALS | 5.5G FAT | 1.1G SAT FAT | 20.9G CARBS | 8.8G SUGARS | 9.1G FIBER | 3.3G PROTEIN | 640MG SODIUM

DESSERTS AND SNACKS

POACHED RHUBARB WITH EDIBLE FLOWERS

There is no need to add sugar to this pretty rhubarb dessert, because the addition of elderflowers provides its own sweetness.

SERVES: 4
PREP: 10 MINS COOK: 6 MINS

1 pound 2 ounces tender red rhubarb
juice of ½ lemon
1¼ tablespoons acacia or other mild honey
flowers from 3 elderflower heads, rinsed, or
1 tablespoon dried elderflowers (available online)
2 tablespoons edible flowers, such as elderflowers,
lavender flowers, and violet flowers
or pink rose petals, to serve

1. Cut the rhubarb stalks into 2¾-inch pieces and arrange in a large, lidded skillet in one layer.

2. Combine the lemon juice, honey, ½ cup of hot water, and the elderflowers from the three heads in a large heatproof bowl. Pour this mixture over the rhubarb and bring to a simmer over medium–low heat. Put the lid on and simmer for 3 minutes, then turn the rhubarb pieces over and simmer for an additional 2 minutes, or until the rhubarb is just tender when pierced with a sharp knife. Using a slotted spoon, transfer the fruit to serving bowls.

3. Stir the liquid to reduce to a syrupy consistency and pass through a strainer to remove the cooked elderflower petals. Spoon the syrup over the rhubarb and decorate with elder, lavender, or violet flowers or rose petals to serve.

RHUBARB RULES
Rhubarb is low in calories and is a well-known laxative, as well as being a good source of calcium and vitamin C.

PER SERVING: 50 CALS | 0.2G FAT | 0.1G SAT FAT | 12G CARBS | 7.2G SUGARS | 2.5G FIBER | 1.2G PROTEIN | TRACE SODIUM

CACAO AND AVOCADO MOUSSE WITH CINNAMON BERRIES

Here's an unusual dessert that you definitely do not have to feel guilty for enjoying—it is full of healthy ingredients and sweetened with agave nectar instead of sugar.

SERVES: 4
PREP: 4¼ HOURS COOK: NONE

2 ripe avocados, halved and pitted
⅔ cup cacao powder
¼ cup agave nectar
seeds from ½ vanilla bean
½ teaspoon chili powder
¼ cup coconut milk
⅓ cup hulled wild or small strawberries
⅓ cup fresh raspberries
½ teaspoon ground cinnamon

1. Scoop the avocado flesh into a large bowl and mash lightly with fork. Stir in the cacao powder, agave nectar, vanilla seeds, and chili powder. Blend thoroughly with an immersion blender until the mixture is thick and smooth. Stir in the coconut milk and blend again.

2. Spoon the avocado mixture into ramekins (individual ceramic dishes) or small, stemmed glasses. Cover with plastic wrap and chill for at least 4 hours.

3. Decorate the avocado mousses evenly with the berries and sprinkle the cinnamon over each dish. Serve immediately.

CACAO RICHNESS
Cacao is rich in antioxidants, including flavonoids and catechins—its antioxidant level is higher even than green and black tea, and cacao is also packed with fiber.

PER SERVING: 249 CALS | 15.8G FAT | 5.1G SAT FAT | 32.9G CARBS | 17G SUGARS | 11.7G FIBER | 4.9G PROTEIN | TRACE SODIUM

CHILLED MELON BREEZE SMOOTHIE BOWL

This smoothie bowl will chill you out and cool you down on a hot summer's day. This would also work as an appetizer or breakfast dish.

SERVES: 1
PREP: 10 MINS COOK: NONE

2 cups peeled and seeded green melon
1 cucumber
¼ cup chopped fresh mint, plus a sprig to garnish
1 cup chilled coconut water

1. Chop the melon and cucumber and put into a blender or food processor.

2. Add the mint, pour in the coconut water, and blend until smooth and creamy.

3. Serve immediately or chill in the refrigerator. Stir just before serving, garnished with a sprig of mint.

MELON MAGIC
A melon contains 92 percent water, which keeps the kidneys working well. All melons are rich in vitamin B6, potassium, and soluble fiber.

PER SERVING: 194 CALS | 1.3G FAT | 0.5G SAT FAT | 44G CARBS | 33.8G SUGARS | 7.4G FIBER | 5.4G PROTEIN | 240MG SODIUM

COCONUT MILK AND STRAWBERRY ICE CREAM

Everyone loves ice cream, but it can be loaded with a ton of processed sugar.
This version is made with just three wholesome ingredients.

SERVES: 6
PREP: 25 MINS FREEZE: 6 HOURS

2 cups hulled and halved strawberries
1²/₃ cups coconut milk
¹/₃ cup honey
crushed hazelnuts, to serve (optional)

1. Puree the strawberries in a food processor or blender, then press through a fine-mesh strainer set over a mixing bowl to remove the seeds.

2. Add the coconut milk and honey to the strawberry puree and whisk together.

3. Pour the mixture into a large roasting pan to a depth of ³/₄ inch, cover the top of the pan with plastic wrap, then freeze for about 2 hours, until just set.

4. Scoop back into the food processor or blender and process again until smooth to break down the ice crystals. Pour into a plastic container or 9 x 5-inch loaf pan lined with nonstick parchment paper. Place the lid on the plastic container or fold the paper over the ice cream in the loaf pan. Return to the freezer for 3–4 hours, or until firm enough to scoop.

5. Serve immediately or let stand in the freezer overnight or until needed. Thaw at room temperature for 15 minutes to soften slightly, then scoop into individual dishes and top with crushed hazelnuts to serve, if using.

STRAWBERRY SUNSHINE
Natural sugars found in strawberries are absorbed more slowly than processed sugars. Strawberries are also an excellent source of vitamin C, manganese, and fiber.

PER SERVING: 198 CALS | 14.4G FAT | 12.6G SAT FAT | 19.3G CARBS | 16.9G SUGARS | 1.5G FIBER | 1.9G PROTEIN | TRACE SODIUM

RAW TAHINI CARAMEL SQUARES

Rich in nuts, cacao, and fruit, these truly delicious squares are great for a healthy dessert or snack.

MAKES: 16 SQUARES
PREP: 20 MINS, PLUS SOAKING AND CHILLING   COOK: NONE

CRUST
½ cup dried apple pieces
8 pitted medjool dates
⅔ cup almonds
1 teaspoon coconut oil
¼ teaspoon sea salt

CARAMEL
⅔ cup raw cashew nuts
5 pitted medjool dates
¼ cup coconut oil
2 tablespoons light tahini
3 tablespoons maple syrup

CHOCOLATE TOPPING
¼ cup coconut oil
¼ cup maple syrup
2 teaspoons date syrup
¼ cup raw cacao powder
½ teaspoon vanilla bean seeds

1. Line a 6-inch square pan with parchment paper, making sure the paper overhangs the edges by 2 inches.

2. To make the crust, soak the apple pieces in water for 5 minutes, then drain and add to a food processor with the remaining crust ingredients. Pulse until the dates and nuts are finely chopped and the mixture is sticky. Spoon the mixture into the bottom of the prepared pan and press down evenly to cover it. Put into the freezer to chill for at least 15 minutes.

3. To make the caramel, pulse the nuts and dates in a food processor until you have a smooth mixture. Add the oil, tahini, and maple syrup and process again to a smooth paste. If necessary, to make a paste of dropping consistency, add 1–2 tablespoons of water and process again. Smooth the caramel on top of the crust in the pan and return to the freezer for 1 hour.

4. To make the chocolate topping, heat the oil and syrups in a small saucepan over medium-low heat and stir in the cacao powder and vanilla seeds. Keep stirring until you have a glossy sauce. Pour it over the cold caramel and return to the freezer for 1 hour, or until the topping is firm.

5. Remove the mixture from the pan by gripping the overhanging paper. Put onto a cutting board and cut into 16 squares with a sharp knife. Serve or store in an airtight container in the refrigerator for up to seven days.

PER SQUARE: 232 CALS | 14G FAT | 7.1G SAT FAT | 27.7G CARBS | 21.4G SUGARS | 3.3G FIBER | 3.5G PROTEIN | 40MG SODIUM

COCONUT, CACAO, AND HAZELNUT TRUFFLES

These small treats are just bursting with a nutritious mix of vital minerals, vitamins, protein, and raw ingredients.

MAKES: 20 TRUFFLES
PREP: 25 MINS COOK: NONE

2/3 cup unblanched hazelnuts
1/2 cup cacao nibs, plus 1 tablespoon for coating
6 dried soft figs, coarsely chopped
1/3 cup dry unsweetened coconut,
plus 2 tablespoons for coating
1 tablespoon maple syrup
finely grated zest and juice of 1/2 small orange

1. Add the hazelnuts and the 1/2 cup cacao nibs to a food processor and process until finely chopped.

2. Add the figs, the 1/3 cup coconut, maple syrup, and orange zest and juice to the processor and process until finely chopped and the mixture has come together in a ball.

3. Scoop the mixture out of the food processor, then cut into 20 even pieces. Roll into small balls in your hands.

4. Finely chop the extra cacao nibs, then mix with the extra coconut on a sheet of nonstick parchment paper on a plate. Roll the truffles, one at a time, in the cacao and coconut mixture, then arrange in a small plastic container. Store in the refrigerator for up to three days.

RAW CACAO
Unlike cocoa powder, which is made by roasting cacao at high temperatures, raw cacao is cold-pressed to retain more minerals and antioxidants.

PER TRUFFLE: 79 CALS | 5.5G FAT | 2.4G SAT FAT | 6.3G CARBS | 4.8G SUGARS | 1.7G FIBER | 1.4G PROTEIN | TRACE SODIUM

RAW CHOCOLATE, CHERRY, AND ALMOND FUDGE BITES

These little cherry-filled bites are easy and quick to make—they also contain no added sugar, good-for-you cacao, and make an ideal gift!

MAKES: 35 PIECES
PREP: 10 MINS, PLUS CHILLING   COOK: NONE

⅓ cup unsweetened almond butter
⅓ cup coconut oil
⅔ cup raw cacao powder
⅓ cup plus 2 teaspoons honey
¼ teaspoon sea salt
seeds from ½ vanilla bean
⅓ cup dried cherries

1. Blend the almond butter and coconut oil in a food processor for a few seconds to combine. Add the cacao powder and blend again.

2. Stir in the honey, salt, and vanilla seeds and blend again. Stir in the dried cherries. Do not blend again once the cherries have gone in.

3. Line a shallow pan or tray that is about 5 x 4 inches with parchment paper, making sure the paper overhangs the edges by at least 2 inches. Spoon the mixture into the pan and level the surface. Put the pan into the freezer for about an hour, or until firm.

4. Remove the fudge from the pan by gripping the overhanging paper. Put onto a cutting board and, using a sharp knife, cut into five slices lengthwise. Then cut each slice into seven squares. Serve or store in an airtight container in the refrigerator.

CHANGE OF PACE
For a variation, try the same recipe but use cashew butter instead of the almond butter and chopped dried goldenberries instead of the cherries.

PER PIECE: 55 CALS | 3.8G FAT | 1.9G SAT FAT | 5.9G CARBS | 3.9G SUGARS | 1.1G FIBER | 1G PROTEIN | TRACE SODIUM

RAW DATE
AND COCONUT BARS

*These chunky, nutty bars get the most out of the raw ingredients.
They are perfect for keeping you energized at work all afternoon long.*

MAKES: 12 BARS
PREP: 15 MINS, PLUS CHILLING COOK: NONE

16 medjool dates, halved and pitted
½ cup unblanched almonds
½ cup cashew nut pieces
2 tablespoons plus 1 teaspoon chia seeds
2 tablespoons maca
seeds from 1 vanilla bean
⅓ cup dry unsweetened coconut
½ cup coarsely chopped unblanched hazelnuts
¼ cup pecan pieces

1. Add the dates, almonds ,and cashew pieces to a food processor and process until finely chopped.

2. Add the chia seeds, maca, and vanilla seeds, then process until the mixture binds together into a coarse ball.

3. Tear off two sheets of nonstick parchment paper, put one on the work surface, and sprinkle it with half the coconut. Put the date ball on top, then press into a coarsely shaped rectangle with your fingertips. Cover with the second sheet of paper and roll out to a 10 x 8–inch rectangle. Lift off the top piece of paper, sprinkle with the remaining coconut, the hazelnuts, and pecan nuts, then cover again with the paper and briefly roll with a rolling pin to press the nuts into the date mixture.

4. Loosen the top paper, then transfer the date mixture, still on the bottom paper, to a tray and chill for 3 hours or overnight, until firm.

5. Remove the top paper, cut the date mixture into 12 pieces, peel off the bottom paper, then pack into a plastic container, layering with pieces of parchment paper to keep them separate. Store in the refrigerator for up to three days.

DATE DARLINGS

Dates are high in fiber and are a good source of potassium, calcium, iron, phosphorus, and magnesium. They are thought to help with intestinal problems.

PER BAR: 224 CALS | 11G FAT | 2G SAT FAT | 31.6G CARBS | 23.1G SUGARS | 5.4G FIBER | 4.2G PROTEIN | TRACE SODIUM

ROASTED SPICY EDAMAME AND CRANBERRIES

Frozen edamame or young soybeans make a healthy, protein-packed snack, and their high levels of fiber keep you feeling fuller for longer.

SERVES: 4
PREP: 15 MINS, PLUS COOLING COOK: 15 MINS

2⅓ cups frozen edamame beans
2-inch piece fresh ginger, peeled and finely grated
1 teaspoon Sichuan peppercorns, coarsely crushed
1 tablespoon tamari
1 tablespoon olive oil
3 star anise
¼ cup dried cranberries

1. Preheat the oven to 350°F. Put the beans into a roasting pan, then sprinkle with the ginger and peppercorns, drizzle with tamari and oil, and mix together.

2. Tuck the star anise in among the beans, then roast, uncovered, in the preheated oven for 15 minutes.

3. Stir in the cranberries and let cool. Spoon into a small jar and eat within 12 hours.

EDAMAME ENERGY
Edamame are versatile and pack a much bigger nutritional punch than frozen peas.

PER SERVING: 182 CALS | 9.2G FAT | 1.1G SAT FAT | 12.7G CARBS | 7.4G SUGARS | 4.4G FIBER | 11.2G PROTEIN | 200MG SODIUM

MIXED SEED CRACKERS

If you've never made your own crackers before, you can't go wrong with these crunchy treats, made with loads of nutritious seeds and no grain at all.

MAKES: 30 CRACKERS
PREP: 10 MINS, PLUS SOAKING AND COOLING
COOK: 1 HOUR 20 MINS

⅓ cup chia seeds
½ cup flaxseed
½ cup pumpkin seeds
½ cup sunflower seeds
2 tablespoons ground flaxseed with berries
1 tablespoon sesame seeds
1 teaspoon sea salt
2 teaspoons nutritional yeast flakes
½ teaspoon dried rosemary
½ teaspoon dried thyme

1. Put the chia seeds and flaxseed into a large bowl. Add 1 cup of cold water, stir, and set aside for 15 minutes. Preheat the oven to 275°F.

2. Stir in all of the other ingredients and mix well to combine. Line a baking pan that is about 11 x 15 inches with parchment paper. Pour the cracker mixture onto the parchment paper and spread the mixture out evenly across the whole of the pan—you can use your clean fingers or the back of a large spoon to do this.

3. When the mixture is spread evenly, make four evenly spaced lengthwise scores into only the top half of the mix. Make five evenly spaced widthwise scores so that you have an outline for 30 rectangular crackers. Place the baking pan in the center of the preheated oven and bake for 45 minutes.

4. Take the pan out and turn the cracker sheet over, using two large flat spatulas. (If this is difficult, cut the cracker sheet into two down one of the premade scores, using a large sharp knife, before turning). Return the pan to the oven for an additional 35 minutes.

5. Turn the cracker sheet out onto a wooden board (a glass or metal surface will tend to make the crackers break when you're cutting them) and, while still warm, cut into 30 crackers through the score marks. Place on a wire rack to cool for at least 30 minutes, then serve or store in an airtight container.

PER CRACKER: 66 CALS | 5.3G FAT | 0.6G SAT FAT | 3.1G CARBS | 0.2G SUGARS | 2.3G FIBER | 2.7G PROTEIN | 80MG SODIUM

ROASTED KALE CHIPS

Kale's flavor becomes wonderfully intense when the leaves are roasted. These chips are perfect on their own or sprinkled over soup.

SERVES: 4
PREP: 20 MINS COOK: 10–12 MINS

9 ounces kale
2 tablespoons olive oil
½ teaspoon sugar
½ teaspoon sea salt
2 tablespoons toasted slivered almonds, to garnish

1. Preheat the oven to 300°F. Remove the thick stems and rib in the center from the kale (leaving about 2½ cups trimmed leaves). Rinse and dry thoroughly with paper towels. Tear into bite-size pieces and put into a bowl with the oil and sugar, then toss well.

2. Spread about half of the leaves in a single layer in a large roasting pan, spaced well apart. Sprinkle with half of the salt and roast on the bottom rack of the preheated oven for 4 minutes.

3. Stir the leaves, then turn the pan so the back is at the front. Roast for an additional 1–2 minutes, or until the leaves are crisp and just slightly browned at the edges. Repeat with the remaining leaves and salt. Sprinkle the kale chips with the slivered almonds and serve immediately. These are best eaten on the day they are made.

KALE KARMA
Kale boasts plenty of calcium, vitamin C, the B-group vitamins, and beta-carotene. It also provides high levels of iron, making this a great vegetable for vegetarians.

PER SERVING: 119 CALS | 9.7G FAT | 1.1G SAT FAT | 6.8G CARBS | 2.1G SUGARS | 2.7G FIBER | 3.6G PROTEIN | 320MG SODIUM

Desserts and snacks

FIBER-RICH FRUIT AND NUT TRAIL MIX

Trail mix must be an all-time favorite snack, and this recipe is loaded with energy-boosting and fiber-rich fruit, nuts, and seeds.

SERVES: 12
PREP: 10 MINS COOK: NONE

½ cup chopped dried apricots
½ cup dried cranberries
⅔ cup roasted cashew nuts
¾ cup shelled hazelnuts
⅔ cup shelled Brazil nuts, halved
¾ cup slivered almonds
¼ cup toasted pumpkin seeds
¼ cup sunflower seeds
¼ cup toasted pine nuts

1. Put all the ingredients into an airtight container, close the lid, and shake several times.

2. Shake the container before each opening, then reseal. This mix will stay fresh for up to two weeks if tightly sealed.

CASHEW CRAZY
Cashew nuts have a lower fat content than most nuts, and most of their fat is unsaturated fatty acids. They also have a high antioxidant content.

PER SERVING: 267 CALS | 21.2G FAT | 2.8G SAT FAT | 17.1G CARBS | 9.8G SUGARS | 3.6G FIBER | 7.2G PROTEIN | TRACE SODIUM

INDEX